Abraham, Sarah, Hagar, and Us:
Using Family Systems Therapy to Understand and Dismantle Oppression

Janaki Spickard Keeler

Pendle Hill Pamphlet 478

About the Author:

Janaki Spickard Keeler, LCSW, is a writer, family therapist, mother, and lifelong Quaker. She is the editor of the Pendle Hill pamphlets and serves as coordinator of the Friends Counseling Service of Philadelphia Yearly Meeting. She is a member of Chestnut Hill Friends Meeting in Philadelphia. This pamphlet originated as part of her (self-imposed) final project for the inaugural class of *Participating in God's Power*, a ministry of the School of the Spirit.

The author thanks Shulamith Clearbridge, Maya Wright, Ellen Deacon, Phil Anthony, Kody Hersh, Melissa Bennett, Amey Hutchinson, the *Participating in God's Power* cohort, and Jim Spickard for their feedback and help in developing this essay.

Editor: Anna McCormally

Editorial Assistant: Carol Holmes Alpern

Publications Staff: Janaki Spickard Keeler

Designer: John Gummere

Cover Image from page 127 of "Delightful stories; or, Home talks out of the Wonderful book." (1888). Public domain.

Requests for permission to quote should be addressed to:
Pendle Hill Publications, 338 Plush Mill Road, Wallingford, PA 19086-6023

Email: publications@pendlehill.org

ISBN 978-0-87574-478-0

December 2022: 1,500

Abraham, Sarah, Hagar, and Us:
Using Family Systems Therapy to Understand and Dismantle Oppression

My father tells a story of when I was two or three years old. We were in the kitchen and, while he was distracted making dinner, I did something—no one remembers what. Catching sight of me, he yelled, "Janaki, DON'T DO THAT!" I immediately turned around and yelled at the cat.

It's a tale as old as time. People unload their negative emotions, often onto those nearest to them. And it's telling that I unloaded mine onto the cat, the only being in the room with less power than me, instead of yelling back at my father. Fortunately, the cat was not upset.

I am a therapist, with a specialization in family therapy. Family therapy is peacemaking work. Families can be bastions of strength and resilience, *and* they can be the place where we are dealt our deepest wounds. Sometimes both of these things are true at the same time. Many of the issues that come up in family therapy are around power: who has it and who uses it, and to what effect. Parents generally have more power than children, for example, which is normal and right if the power is not abused and if it is used in service of all members of the family. Power is not inherently destructive or wrong, but it is, well, *powerful.* When power is used well in families, happiness and balance are usually the fruits. Misused, power can do a lot of damage. In this pamphlet, I will explore how the use and misuse of power at the family level is mirrored at the societal level as well—and how the tools of family systems therapy and our Quaker tradition can help us heal.

When trauma and misfortune come along, unhealthy power dynamics in families often come to the fore. As therapists, we often say "Hurt people hurt people." While not all people who experience trauma go on to harm others, many—perhaps all—of those who cause the most harm have histories with trauma, particularly early in their lives. That is especially true of those who have not found a way to deal with their trauma in a non-harmful manner. If those people are in positions of power, the damage they do can be hard to stop. And those they hurt may not know how to deal with the pain and may go on to hurt others.

This is the lens through which I approach the world and the healing work of family therapy: who has power, who uses their power, and whether they use it constructively or destructively.

Now let's talk about faith. For years, I have wrestled with the story of Abraham's near-sacrifice of his son Isaac in Genesis 17–22. That story is in many ways a perfect illustration of the harm the misuse of power can do. It is also a story with layers, and a story with complex family dynamics that when brought to the surface can help us see more deeply into our lives today. It is the story of the ways in which each adult member of the family—Abraham, Sarah, and Hagar—is both traumatized by and complicit in the violence committed. In this essay, I will peel back the layers of the story Jewish tradition calls the *Akedah,* which most Christians know as the *Binding of Isaac.* Using the lens of family systems therapy, we will see what it can teach us about faithfulness, about the use and misuse of power, and about the challenges of racial justice, predatory capitalism, and systemic violence in our society today.

The Binding of Isaac

God had made a covenant with Abraham that his descendants would be as uncountable as the stars (Genesis 15:5–6) and that they would be given the land of Canaan. Nonetheless, decades passed and his wife Sarah was barren. When Sarah was ninety years old, God told them that Sarah would bear a son. Both Abraham and Sarah laughed; this was clearly impossible. But Sarah gave birth to Isaac, whose name meant "laughter."

The boy grew. In Genesis 22, we are told God tested Abraham. He told Abraham to take his son to the land of Moriah and offer him as a burnt offering on the mountain there. Abraham and Isaac traveled to Moriah and prepared the burnt offering together. Isaac asked his father where the lamb for the offering was, and Abraham told him God would provide the lamb.

Abraham built an altar and bound his son, laying him on top of the wood and drawing his knife to kill him. But the angel of the Lord called to him from heaven, telling him not to harm the child: "For now I know that you fear God, since you have not withheld your son, your only son, from me" (Genesis 22:12, NRSV). Abraham saw a ram caught in a thicket and offered it as a burnt offering instead of his son.

The angel of the Lord called again from heaven, saying, "By myself I have sworn, says the Lord: Because you have done this, and have not withheld your son, your only son, I will indeed bless you, and I will make your offspring as numerous as the stars of heaven and as the sand that is on the seashore. And your offspring shall possess the gate of their enemies, and by your offspring shall all the nations of the earth gain blessing for themselves, because you have obeyed my voice" (Genesis 22:16–18). Abraham and Isaac then went to Beersheba, where Abraham lived thereafter.

The classic interpretation of this story is we must always do what God asks of us, even if it will cost us everything we value. Traditionally, Abraham is lauded as a righteous man of faith, someone to emulate. He is the perfect patriarch, faithful to God unto extremis.

Personally, however, I find this story horrific. Since the birth of my own son—long-awaited and prayed-for, and something of a miracle child himself—I find it even more incomprehensible. To believe that God is asking for this act of violence as a test of faith makes me physically ill, and Abraham's passive acceptance is even worse. It would be easy to reject this story, and reject the Christian faith tradition it comes from. At the same time, the story of Abraham's near-sacrifice of Isaac is part of my heritage, both as a member of the Religious Society of Friends and as a citizen. My country was founded by Christians who, taking guidance from stories like this one, reenacted age-old narratives of power through genocide, slavery, and exploitation.

Can I worship a God who can ask Abraham to murder his own son? How do I find that of God in what Abraham was willing to do? How do I come to terms with a religion and a country rooted in violence and the abuse of power? In my therapy work, I help people change the narratives they tell about themselves, in order to break cycles of trauma and abuse. Doesn't our ailing and addicted world need something similar? Is there a way to redeem the stories our society tells? Do we need to drop the story of Abraham and Isaac from our spiritual repertoire, or is there a truth in it that a deeper reading can reveal?

Consider that Abraham's willingness to sacrifice his son is akin to the way early Quakers approached their faith. Early Friends, who strove to live lives in total accord with the instructions of the Inward Christ, spoke of "living in the Cross"—that is, like Jesus, making the decision to follow God's will even unto death.[1] Friends have taken this seriously over the centuries. When they hear God's call, Friends have been willing to sacrifice everything—reputation, property, freedom, livelihood, family relationships, even their own lives—to follow faithfully. Many early Quakers ended up in prison. Some were executed for following their faith. Later, Friends working to abolish slavery faced the backlash of the society around them, both socially and legally. More recently, Friends who refused to fight in wars were often jailed or sent to workcamps, enduring terrible conditions to live by their inward conviction that killing is not in accordance with a life in the Spirit. There's something beautiful and powerful in their example, and—dare I say it?—something worth emulating. There's a reason we're drawn to the fire of George Fox and early Friends, and to the Friends who live their lives in the Cross today. They've tapped into a vein of spiritual power that is stronger and more authentic in them because they've chosen to cooperate with it, to work in tandem through submission of the will. Is this not like Abraham's faithfulness?

Yet there's another dimension to the story beyond what these faithful Friends saw, something I could see only because of my family therapy training. In the vocabulary of family systems theory, which holds that individuals are not solitary actors and their actions and choices are inseparable from their network of relationships, we would call the *Binding of Isaac* an "enactment." It is a microcosm of larger family dynamics and even societal dynamics illustrated in a single defining event, and it can teach us much when carefully examined. Let's see what unlayering this story reveals.

Abraham

Here are two different readings of what God and Abraham are doing in this story.

1.

I have never been satisfied with the idea that God is testing Abraham's faith—or more importantly, his obedience. I don't hold with a faith of blind obedience. For me, it's important to discern whether the voice I hear is really God talking—and if so, whether this is a god worth following.

However, Friends pastor Micah Bales has a take on this story that has influenced me greatly in my wrestling:

> When I hear this story, I'm forced to ask myself: What does it mean to sacrifice my Isaac? . . . Isaac is not merely a beloved child. He is the instrument of God's promise. . . . Without Isaac, Abraham has nothing to hold onto, nothing to assure him that God really cares for him and has a plan for him. . . . When God tells Abraham to kill his son Isaac, he's essentially asking Abraham this: "Do you trust me enough to let go of everything in this world that connects us? Do you love me more than my gifts, more than my promises, more than my presence in your life?"
>
> This is a story about Abraham seeking a truer, more authentic faith. Beyond pleading and promises. Beyond rewards. Abraham gives himself to God unconditionally—even if it means the loss of everything else, including his ideas about God.[2]

If we take this story as an invitation to self-examination, we're being called into a deeper faith. We're being invited beyond our earthly and limited projections of what the Divine is. Instead of treating our faith in God as a transaction, we are being called to truly partner with God, a partnership that requires complete surrender. We are being offered a chance to take a step over the edge of the cliff and trust that Love will hold us up. We can live the paradox of a world where pain and suffering and oppression permeate everything, and yet also—against all odds—discover that there is a hope at the heart of the universe, a hope that will meet us and sustain us in the depths of our pain: a promise that love is never wasted.

Micah Bales offers the query, "What are we being called to surrender, so that we can be more fully embraced by God?" This query begins to crack open the story for me. What things do I hold dear? What do I cling tightly to, afraid I'd be undone by the losing thereof? Could these things actually be blocking me from embracing the Divine? What parts of myself and the way I am in the world keep me separate and isolated—from God and from other human beings?

We can draw on our tradition for help with this surrender and self-examination. Quakers have long had a spiritual practice of holding our lives up to the Light, as described and revived by Rex Ambler.[3] The early Quakers found this was not at all a comfortable or reassuring practice. Under the bright Inward Light, they unearthed parts of themselves they perhaps would rather have not known, parts that were not aligned with the Spirit. They stood convicted, awakened to the sin that kept them from true communion with the Divine.

Margaret Fell wrote about the experience:

> Now, Friends, deal plainly with yourselves, and let the eternal Light search you, and try you, for the good of your souls. For this will deal plainly with you. It will rip you up, and lay you open, and make all manifest which lodges in you; the secret subtlety of the enemy of your souls, this eternal searcher and trier will make manifest. Therefore all to this come, and by this be searched, and judged, and led and guided. For to this you must stand or fall.[4]

The sins revealed by the Light can be subtler than the list of Thou Shalt Nots. They can be things like hypocrisy, easy to see in others but difficult to recognize in oneself. They can be an ungenerousness of spirit that colors all one's interactions. They can be insidious: internalized racism, for example, is a sin that many of us in the Religious Society of Friends are finally facing in ourselves. This sin hurts all of us, oppressors and oppressed alike. Participating in a system that props up racism requires us all to alienate our innate tendencies toward empathy and community. Those among us who benefit from racist systems are able to hold onto comfort, wealth, and privilege only by putting up a wall between us and other people, between us and God.

Holding onto a racist status quo comes at the cost of true compassion and community, of recognizing that of God in everyone. In this way, in addition to harming Black and brown people, our racism takes us farther from the Divine. Is not the Abraham story a call to a radical faithfulness that connects us again?

2.

Novelist Dan Simmons, in *The Fall of Hyperion*, suggests a different interpretation of the story of the *Binding of Isaac.* In it, God is testing Abraham, but it's not a test of Abraham's faithfulness. It's a test of Abraham's spiritual maturity.[5]

Up until this time in the Hebrew Bible, the relationship between God and man is one of authority and obedience. Like any parent of a young child, God has had to say "no" a lot to humans for their own good and insist upon their absolute obedience to rules they don't really understand. This is to keep them safe. Parents have a bigger picture than the child does of the consequences of certain actions. When their child runs into the street, that is time for an authoritative, "Janaki, don't DO that!" and unquestioning obedience to that authority so that the child isn't hit by a car. This is a responsible use of power and authority with a child who is still developing the capacity to reason.

But part of parenting is letting your child grow up. There comes a time when the child internalizes the parent's authority and the rules it represents, and starts to understand the concepts of right and wrong without needing an external guide. The child learns not to hit their classmates not because the parent or authority figure says no, but because their internalized morality says it isn't right. Their sense of compassion tells them that hitting others causes pain to both parties. As the child grows up, that internalized moral compass will (hopefully) guide them more than the threat of consequences. The parent-child relationship no longer needs unquestioning obedience and can become more a relationship of equals. The child may even be able to tell parents when the parents are falling short of the lessons they instilled. The child begins to be able to access the Inward Light and let it guide them. In this new stage of maturity, simple obedience is not necessarily the faithful path, not if the child knows that what they are being asked is wrong.

What if, Simmons says, the *Binding of Isaac* isn't about obedience at all? What if God the Father wants to know whether Abraham, his beloved son and a righteous man, is ready for the next stage of their relationship? Whether he's reached a stage of moral development where he can turn to God and say, "Hold on. You want me to do something evil, but you've taught me not to do evil"?

In this reading of the story, Abraham is tested, and he fails the test.

Sarah

Now let's look at the story from Sarah's point of view. It shows us layers that the traditional focus on Abraham misses.

In the *Binding of Isaac*, we have a story in which the man with power disregards all other interests because he believes he is right. Abraham believes he is divinely led. This is a story that every woman I know has experienced: a man who believes he is right, acting without input, and a woman—Sarah—suffering the consequences. Isaac, the powerless child, also suffers. What would it be like to know that your father would willingly murder you because his God told him to?

Imagine if Abraham had been a Quaker. Imagine if he had said to his faith community, "God is asking me to kill my son. What do you think?" I can picture the women in my meeting saying to him, "You have no right to do this. Isaac is not yours to sacrifice." Abraham, like too many Bible readers, thinks this story is about him. But he is a single element of a family system.

Even before I became a mother, I wondered how Sarah, the matriarch who gave birth to the miracle child and his laughter, reacted to her husband's willingness to sacrifice their child. In a patriarchal society no doubt Abraham felt he had more rights over his son and thus his son's life than Sarah did. But the act of carrying a child in your own body, building the child cell by cell in a mysterious yet instinctual process, giving birth, feeding from your body, giving and giving and giving: that creates an almost unbreakable bond. Your child is *yours* and always will be, even as he grows up and grows independent. Laws and patriarchs may think that they own the child, but there is a deeper law in the heart that almost every person who bears a child knows.

Losing a child is one of the most singularly heartbreaking and difficult experiences a person can go through. It often breaks up families. My own family and each of us in it fractured after the violent death of my stepsister Rachel. So I am certain that Sarah, no matter how faithful she was personally, would never understand God's request or Abraham's willingness. She would see it as betrayal, and as murder.

I am not the first to have seen this. Quaker author and minister Philip Gulley spoke to my soul when he wrote about this:

> I grew up hearing all these wonderful things about Abraham, but any man who'd do that to a child is flat out insane, I don't care what voice he thought he heard. Apparently, his wife Sarah was infuriated, because afterwards they stopped living together. She lived in Hebron in the land of Canaan, and he lived in Beersheba. They died apart and estranged. . . .
>
> One more instance in the long and tragic history of men behaving as if women had no say. Sarah would not stand for it. . . . I like Sarah. . . . I like that in her old age, with few resources at her disposal, she was able to say, "I would rather live alone than with a man who would place our child on an altar and slice him open."
>
> I am done with Abraham and his god. I am standing with the god of Sarah, . . . who long ago whispered in her ear, "There is a better life in Hebron. Let us go there together."[6]

I identify with Sarah. I think many women do. Many of us have had the experience of a man misusing his power in ways that hurt us: sometimes violently, sometimes subtly. So much of my experience of the world involves men doing things that do not take my well-being, rights, or emotions into account. I project my own anger and outrage onto Sarah. How could she fail to scream internally when Abraham was willing to take away the baby boy she wanted for so long, enduring ninety years of society telling her she was a failure for being barren?

Growing up and seeing the overt and covert sexism that saturates our society, I discovered that there is an entire system in place that privileges the male voice in ways large and small. As Gulley says,

> The vestiges of Abraham's god are still with us. . . . That god is worshiped by those who would compel a woman to bear a child she had no say in creating, then do nothing to assist her . . . when fathers make war that cost[s] mothers their children . . . when single mothers toil in two or three jobs and still cannot support their families . . . when men do what they wish while women suffer what they must.

But that of God within us knows the truth. The Light can help us discern what is really holy and what is sin, what is hypocrisy. Indeed, I too want to embrace the God of Sarah that Gulley describes. Sarah could clearly see her husband's sin of blind obedience. This man had bargained with God when God planned to destroy Sodom and Gomorrah, arguing that if He would spare the city for the sake of fifty righteous men, He should spare it for the sake of ten (Genesis 18:16–33). And yet Abraham said nary a word when it came to her beloved son. Her husband, the person she should have been able to count on to never harm a single hair on her baby's head, made a decision without a second thought. Abraham was a righteous man, we are told. She trusted him. He betrayed that trust.

And I imagine she felt that God had betrayed that trust as well.

I can imagine Sarah learning to cry silently in the night because even tears are a challenge to the patriarchy. I can imagine her thinking, *I've done everything right! For years and years and years I've been faithful, I've stuffed down my feelings, I've been subservient, I acted for the good of the family even when it hurt me. How can this be what I end up with?* For a long time, I saw Sarah as an innocent victim, a sacrifice Abraham was willing to make.

If only the narrative were that simple.

Hagar

What I missed in my initial struggles with this story was its context. There's a lot more that happened with Abraham and Sarah and their family that I had overlooked in my preoccupation with the traumatic event of the *Binding of Isaac.*[7] My years as a therapist should have taught me this; it is rare that extreme behaviors—such as attempting to kill your child—happen only once. They are generally part of a pattern of extreme behaviors, as family systems reenact the same moments of trauma over and over again, searching for a different result but without the skills to find one.

In the next layer of the story, we have to ask: Was Sarah actually an innocent victim? What power did she have and how did she use it? What trauma did Sarah create? And for whom? To see this, we have to revisit Sarah's experience before Isaac's birth.

God promised Abraham that his descendants would be as numerous as the stars. And God didn't grant Sarah a child until she was ninety years old. They waited for decades. I imagine Sarah, worn out with disappointment, coming to a realization that God promised *Abraham* descendants; God didn't promise *her* descendants.

Sarah lived in a patriarchal culture. Her most important duty was to Abraham's family, and the number one priority was to bear children—sons, specifically. As the years passed and she became an old woman, I can only imagine her feelings. Even in my culture where women without children have value, it was easy for me to feel broken, guilty, and worthless while struggling with infertility. Sarah must have been devastated.

Sarah, like all women in patriarchal cultures, knew how to sacrifice, how to put the good of the family above her own good. It doesn't surprise me that she put her own feelings aside to assure Abraham's legacy. She had practice. In Genesis 12, we hear how she and Abraham went to Egypt during a famine. Because she was so beautiful, Abraham feared he would be killed, so they put it about that he was her brother.[8] Sure enough, Pharaoh saw her beauty and took her for a wife, "and for her sake he dealt well with Abram; and he had sheep, oxen, male donkeys, male and female slaves, female donkeys, and camels" (Genesis 12:16). In other words, Sarah's consent over who did what with her body did not matter in her culture. She may even, to save her sanity, have told herself she was *willing* to be Pharaoh's "wife," and she parlayed her position into wealth for the family. Rape often works this way: a woman is given a "choice" between being raped violently or raped less violently, maybe given some sort of reward for her cooperation, and when she chooses the latter her rapist tells himself that it is not rape. And often she will believe that herself, because it's easier to avoid dealing with a trauma if you don't let yourself believe that a trauma happened at all.

Hurt people hurt people. Sarah, who made sacrifices for her family, who felt a responsibility to assure her husband's destiny, enacted the trauma of her rape on another person. Years before Sarah became pregnant with Isaac, worried she would never conceive, she told her husband to take her slave Hagar to impregnate her. Abraham did, and his first son, Ishmael, was born. Ishmael became Abraham's heir.

The Bible tells us this in a straightforward manner that indicates there is nothing wrong with this plan. Sarah apparently didn't think there was anything wrong with this plan, until Hagar conceived and "looked with contempt on her mistress." This is also translated as "her mistress was lowered in her eyes" (Genesis 16:4). Sarah went to Abraham to protest this "injustice." Abraham gave her permission to deal with it however she wanted to, and Sarah "dealt harshly with her" (Genesis 16:6).

A slave could not say no to the powerful patriarch—or to his wife. Hagar was probably quite young if she was of childbearing age; she was probably a teenager. She was Egyptian, a foreigner with no one to support her: someone of a different racial caste. And it seems the plan of fulfilling God's covenant with Abraham by way of raping a teenager who was powerless to say no, then be subject to the violent jealousy of the woman who had arranged her rape, upset Hagar just as much as it should upset us, because at this point she ran away. She ran out into the desert, where she was liable to die. Things were so bad in the household that even someone who was used to being oppressed and mistreated reached her breaking point. Better to be dead.

An angel of the Lord found her in the desert, and told her to go back and submit to Sarah. It's striking to me what the angel did not say. He didn't promise that things would get better for her. He didn't promise that she'd have protection or redemption. He just shared her part in God's plan: "I will so greatly multiply your offspring that they cannot be counted for multitude. . . . Now you have conceived and shall bear a son; you shall call him Ishmael, for the Lord has given heed to your affliction" (Genesis 16:10–12). *Ishmael* means "God hears." God hears Hagar's pain and accompanies her in it. And in return for the naming of her child, Hagar names God: "You are El-Roi," that is, "God who sees" (Genesis 16:13).

Hagar returned to Abraham and Sarah and bore Ishmael, who became the heir. We don't hear whether anything changed in Sarah's mistreatment of her, but presumably Hagar could take some strength from the knowledge that God saw her oppression and did not turn away from her.

But all was not well. In Genesis 21, we hear how a few years later God's promise to Sarah was fulfilled and she gave birth to Isaac. When Isaac was weaned, Sarah saw him playing with his brother Ishmael, and she realized that under the inheritance law, Isaac would not inherit nearly as much as Ishmael. Again Sarah used her power and position to enact her trauma on Hagar. She told Abraham to cast Hagar and Ishmael out. We are told that this was "very distressing" to Abraham, but he did it. He sent Hagar out into the wilderness with some bread and water and her little son carried on her shoulder.

The water ran out quickly, and Hagar knew she was going to die. She could not bear to see Ishmael die, so she put him under a bush and sat down a bowshot away, and she wept. All of us who have been in despair know what those tears were like.

God heard her, and called from heaven to not be afraid. He bade her to go to her son, again promising that he would make a great nation of him. Then God opened Hagar's eyes and there was a well of water. They would not die. God stayed with them, and Ishmael grew up in the wilderness. His mother eventually found him an Egyptian wife, and he had twelve sons, "princes according to their tribes" (Genesis 25:16), who became the Arab peoples of the Transjordan. Custom has it that many of them became Muslims after the Prophet Muhammad united the Arab tribes in the 600s CE.

* * *

Two women raped. Two children sacrificed. Therapists have a name for the reenactment of trauma in a family system: the *repetition compulsion.* I have witnessed it many times. It's as if the family members are drawn again and again back to an inflection point, trying to get it right. But the unconscious forces are too strong and the trauma is repeated:

The child who endured a father's violent rages grows up to hit his own children.

A mother who was sexually abused as a child and was never believed will not believe her children when they tell her they have been sexually abused.

Parents who were kicked out of their homes as teenagers, forced to grow up and find their way on their own, may do the same thing to their own children because they don't know how to navigate a healthy process of individuation and independence.

Family patterns repeat themselves again and again at crisis points; everyone in the family is retraumatized, but a temporary stability that feels "normal" is regained, and the pull toward that normal is almost inexorable. Healing requires families to identify the destructive pattern, so the work of a family therapist is to bring it to the family's consciousness—and then interrupt it in a way that gives the family new options instead of returning to the unhealthy normal. A family therapist presented with the story of the *Binding of Isaac* might think:

Of course Abraham was willing to sacrifice Isaac without protest. Sarah had trained him to sacrifice a son already. To Abraham, *this was what love required.*

Sarah, acting in response to her own trauma, created the very conditions that would let her be further traumatized down the line. By setting up the attempted murder of her stepson, she was complicit in the attempted murder of her own.

The idea of the innocent victim is getting pretty muddied. If I'm not willing to worship the God of Abraham, how can I worship the God of Sarah?

Us: Bringing It Home

What does this story tell me about my own life and about the society in which I live?

I still find myself identifying with Sarah, both for good and for ill. I feel anguish for the compromises she was forced to make for her family, but when I'm willing to really look at her privilege and her complicity, I see myself. I see a white woman, clinging to her own innocence. And I have clung to that innocence while participating in a social system that has prospered by dominating, oppressing, and often destroying Black, brown, and working people for the sake of richer people's ease.

Sarah wanted her son to prosper, so she arranged for Abraham to drive Hagar and Ishmael into the desert. I have a son who will be going to school in a few years, yet I live in a city that has one of the lowest-performing school districts in the nation. As a therapist, I have watched the city's schools leach the natural joy in learning out of the children I work with, children just a bit older than he. Am I ready to fight my city's school system, seeking better education for all? By the time that fight is won—if it is—my son will be grown and will not have received the education he needs. I find myself thinking about private school (which I cannot afford) or moving to a suburb, which takes my tax dollars away from the city schools that so dearly need them. Neither of these "solutions" improves schools for the city's predominantly Black residents. By using my privilege for my son's betterment, I am complicit in those schools' continued failure to serve the children who need an education every bit as much as he. I am like Sarah, though in my case supporting ongoing racial and economic injustice, not Old Testament patriarchy.

Layers of complicity sustain our society's racial and economic oppression—religious complicity included. God is invoked so often by those in power, in order to justify crimes big and small. Consider that the legal framework for the genocide, enslavement, and theft of land and resources in the New World was built on the Christian church's moral justification that "heathens" did not have the same rights or personhood as Christians. Consider the "God-fearing" men who make policies that imprison children in my country and bomb them in others, thinking that those "other" children do not matter. Consider the generations of men pointing to the Bible as justification for oppressing women, just as they pointed to the Bible as justification for owning slaves, saying that it must not be evil if God didn't object to it.

Sarah and Abraham's treatment of Hagar is very reminiscent of the systematic rape of hundreds of thousands of enslaved women in the pre–Civil War United States—often as a cheap way to enlarge the labor force and thus enrich slaveholder families. That trauma has echoed down the centuries, reinforced by Jim Crow, segregation, and ongoing institutionalized racism. By looking the other way when their husbands raped Black women and forcibly impregnated them, the white wives chose to protect themselves and their family's stability and continued to benefit from the enslaved people's labor. This understanding has haunted me ever since I learned of it: how complicit white women were—and remain—in the evil systems of white supremacy. Those white women most likely clung to the same ideal of innocence that tempts me, pushing the knowledge of the awful sin that benefited them to the back of their minds, telling themselves that those slaves were not people and that slavery was in the Bible so it must be godly. Many very likely took out their jealousy and guilt on enslaved people through further abuse. When we know that trauma perpetuates itself, repeating from generation to generation, is it any wonder that racial trauma is embedded in the United States' very values and institutions?

Is my willingness to escape my city's schools not in effect a choice to sacrifice another person's child? Is this not me, like Sarah, looking out for my son's inheritance at the expense of Hagar's son? It is not too extreme to consider it akin to casting someone out into the desert to die. Children have died in these schools, which cannot even afford to have nurses on staff. Many emerge from them with physical and emotional scars—and little education.

A society that values white middle-class norms and expensive higher education traps non-white and undereducated people in poverty for the rest of their lives. In my work in the city, I've seen how poverty traps whole families in cycles of abuse and addiction—when your daily life is terrible, and resources are scarce, there is little reason to get sober. I've worked with homeless people who are smarter than many of my graduate school colleagues, but who cannot find a way to break out of a rigged system. The public school system—the thing that could have given them a chance to escape—completely failed them.

This is systemic racism, and I am complicit. We can argue about sins of commission versus sins of omission, but both are sins, and both cause harm—to the victims and also to the perpetrators. Participation in systems of oppression that harm other living beings violates those beings, and it also violates the oppressors. What did those enslavers have to do to their own souls, to keep stifling that of God inside them that screamed that what they were doing was evil? What had to break inside for Sarah, for white women who owned slaves, to condone rape? If I send my child to a better school, if I prioritize my own comfort and my child's safety over another's, am I not alienating myself from others, from Divine guidance? Am I not moving myself—and my son—away from the Beloved Community rather than toward it?[9] To continue to live in a system that oppresses, we are forced to cut off our own humanity, whether we are the oppressors or the oppressed.

Family Systems Therapy and Healing Our Society

How, then, do we resist the systems in which we are complicit? How, ultimately, do we contribute to dismantling them? Family systems therapy has some clues that are worth our attention.

At its essence, family systems theory posits that relationships are the site of change, and that everyone in a family or other emotional system has a role in the things that work—and the things that do not. If one person changes, the rest of the family is forced to shift in some way. There is typically real resistance to change, even when things are very dysfunctional, because it often takes a lot of painful flailing to find something that works better for everybody. A family therapist can work with each member of the family to understand what power they have (and don't have) in the situation—how they are complicit in the problem. Then she accompanies the family through the growing pains as they implement their new way of relating.

Family therapy works with broken systems, helping them to heal from the inside out. Our society is pretty broken right now. The only way to heal a family is through helping its members learn to open up, be vulnerable, and have a common goal that prioritizes the needs of all family members—even the needs that do not yet make sense to all of them. My work with families is primarily to help them reconnect to a sense of curiosity about what unmet physical and emotional needs might be motivating problematic behavior and patterns. Then I help the family system meet those needs.

I always keep in mind that polarization is a trauma response, and when I see a polarized family, I know that they are in need of profound healing. When I look at our polarized society, my better self sees that there is trauma that needs to be healed. We are all collectively traumatized by living in systems that are built on oppression and complicity. We'll continue to enact our trauma on others until we can recognize the healing that needs to take place and take steps to make change.

This is not easy work. In my work with families, parents often have to give up cherished dreams of who they want their children to be and what they want their relationship with their kids to look like. Partners have to accept the reality of who the other person really is and what they can really offer. Sometimes people have to change their understanding of what is healthy nurturing and what is enabling—and that can challenge them to give up cherished roles of "the loving one" or "the disciplinarian." They have to face up to the trauma that has affected them. And they have to look closely at how they are complicit in the problems affecting the family system.

Our work of healing our society and ourselves of complicity in oppression involves being willing to surrender much that we cherish because those things stand in the way of fully embracing and being embraced by God. I've had to work on giving up my addiction to believing myself innocent—and also my unwillingness to let others witness my faults and imperfections. We have to give up our conviction that we are right, that we have the whole truth, and that we have answers that work for everyone. We have to give up the premises that built white supremacy and that permeate every part of our legal and social systems—even our religious structures.

We're willing to grow and change for the people we love. Can you imagine what it would look like to be willing to grow and change for love of the whole world?

We have several good examples of what this can look like. John Woolman, our Quaker saint, didn't talk just with other abolitionists: he visited slaveholders and expressed genuine concern for their souls. I have come to recognize this is the only process we have for genuine culture change: a process of being in relationship, standing firm in the Truth, and laboring with others to help them see that Truth. More recently, many Quaker meetings have had to reckon with the acceptance of LGBTQIA folks.[10] Black Quakers have also asked the Society of Friends to recognize its complicity in structural racism and to welcome them as full members of the community, a charge we are still wrestling with.

We are not promised that the process will be easy. Just as God did not promise Hagar that she would be treated better if she returned to Sarah's household, we are not promised that harm will not occur in the process of convincement and conversion. We are not even promised that we will emerge whole and unscathed, as individuals or as the body—whether meeting or Society or nation. Relationships are the site of change, and our best opportunity to find a way to the Truth together, but we can only make the invitation to a deeper faithfulness. We in the LGBTQIA community have had to stand firm in our Truth, deal lovingly with the families and churches and Friends meetings that were not allowing us our full humanity—and be willing to walk away if the family or congregation cannot deal lovingly with us in return and hear the Truth of our hearts. It's important to give others every opportunity, but when an inability to access or follow the promptings of Truth in their own hearts causes relationships and institutions to splinter, that is not the fault of the people who reached out.

Family systems theory teaches us that change and healing only happen when the most powerful members of the family get on board and listen to the less powerful ones. A child can play family peacemaker, but it is a tenuous peace and often detrimental to the child. When families heal, the parents begin to listen to and incorporate the needs of the whole family into the plan for going forward. Peacemaking becomes everyone's priority.

Crucially, the powerful members of the family become willing to undertake the work of change when they realize that the changes they make will benefit themselves as well as the rest of the family. Similarly, our society will not begin to heal until the "victors" realize that their complicity comes at a cost to their own well-being. Oppressive gender roles hurt everybody, not just women, and men freed of patriarchy's strictures can have happier, healthier relationships and emotional lives. Racism lies at the root of the United States' inability to provide basic social safety nets like subsidized child care, universal health care, and welfare and housing supports that other first world countries enjoy, as Heather McGhee illustrates in *The Sum of Us: What Racism Costs Everyone and How We Can Prosper Together.* Even more, complicity in oppression forces us to cut off our instincts toward empathy and community. Healing from our collective traumas benefits *all* of us, materially and spiritually.

If we let it, the Spirit will reveal to us the ways in which we are complicit. The bright Light of Truth convicts us and convinces us that transformation is necessary. Our faith tells us that transformation is possible: that God is leading us to build a new world, free from oppression and complicity.

What this looks like, to me, is building a society where all voices are heard and all needs are valued and prioritized. We do that by reaching out and loving the ones we have cast and who have cast us as enemies. We do that by identifying how we as a society keep reenacting the same old traumas again and again, and making a plan together on how we will break—on a systemic level—the patterns that we have inherited. It takes courage, it takes vulnerability, it takes standing in our Truth, it takes openness to changing and being changed—and it takes asking the Spirit to show us the way forward together. This is what living in the Cross looks like to me in today's world.

What Can Abraham, Sarah, and Hagar Teach Us?

When we look at the story of Abraham and his family, we see some basic human tendencies and shortcomings that are at work in all of us.

When have we, like Abraham, allowed injustice to happen in the name of keeping the peace and maintaining the order of things, as he did when he allowed Sarah to mistreat Hagar and later cast her out?

When have we, like Sarah, prioritized the good of our own children, or our own side, over others?

And when have we, like Abraham, done something wrong—sometimes profoundly wrong—when we thought it was right and Spirit-led, as Abraham did when God asked him to sacrifice Isaac?

But the good news is that when we open ourselves to healing, when we begin to build relationships with the Divine and with other people, another instinct emerges: an instinct toward justice and caring for all people. It is an instinct toward relationship and community. As the early Friends knew, to live truly grounded in the Spirit is to live "in that power which takes away the occasion for all wars" and thus resist that within ourselves which seeks power over others.[11] It is never too late to break the cycles of trauma and oppression that surround us. Healing takes intentional work, but the Spirit is with us and will guide our steps.

There is a final lesson that I take from the story of the *Binding of Isaac*. In Abraham, I see a righteous but deeply flawed man. In Sarah, I see an all-too-human woman acting out of her own trauma. And in Hagar, I see a courageous and spiritual woman fighting to survive. God had a place and a plan for each of them, and even Ishmael and Isaac, the children sacrificed, were set on a path that influenced the entire world. The story is troubling, and I believe we should be troubled by it. But the part of the story that can make me breathe a little easier is that God made use of Abraham even with his shortcomings. A highly imperfect man became the founder of three faiths. What is asked of us is not perfection, but faithfulness and seeking of the Truth. We do not have to be perfect to have a role in the divine plan. We do not have to be perfect to be worthy of having a place in the Beloved Community; we arrive already loved.

A Personal Reflection

There is, as in all things, a personal side to this issue. I find that doing family and social systems work is incredibly difficult. Working with others is hard and requires considerable inner change. This was brought home to me during the 2020 presidential primaries, when I sat in an extended meeting for worship meditating on the *Binding of Isaac* and on the extreme political polarization all around me. In that meeting, the Spirit gave me a message that spoke to my soul:

> There is a ministry building in me, brick by slow brick. It is a ministry of loving enemies, loving neighbors, loving family: all hard things. . . . When we make others into the Other, when we demonize them, when we forget their humanity, we are also doing violence to our own humanity. Hatred, scorn, pushing the other away as inferior to us, as ignorant, as stupid and willful . . . this adds fuel to the fire of dissension rather than seeking a place of common ground on which to build a relationship, to build respect, to build dialogue, to change the other *and let ourselves be changed by the other.* We do not have the whole truth. Each human being was shaped by God and contains a vital part of the truth. We will not have a whole truth until we are in communion, in communication. *Yes,* we have vital truths that *they* need to know. But they too have vital truths for us. We must dwell in our truths *while reaching out* to help them live in and share theirs. And that is the Kingdom of God. Not one side prevailing, but all sides evolving into true righteousness and dwelling in the deeper Truth.

Friends, this ministry makes me deeply uncomfortable, as spending time opening myself to disagreeable others is not what I want to do with my life. Being in relationship with people who do not recognize my full humanity is incredibly hard, and it requires a grounding in my own Truth I don't always have.

So I've let this ministry work on me slowly. Over time, I came to see that the Inward Light had illuminated a piece of my life that is out of divine order. This is an invitation to explore a new way of being, to surrender old stories that are preventing me from living in the Light. Like the early Friends, I need to "take up my Cross" and allow myself to be led by the divine will.

The story of Abraham, Sarah, and Hagar illuminates some deep truths. It is human nature to divide into "us" and "them." We create the Other out of people who are different; we shun and avoid the Other, we project all of our worst qualities onto that Other, and we fear the Other. Male and female, Black and white, Democrat and Republican, rich and poor. It's human nature, but it is an impulse that is dangerous. It's easy to slip into dehumanizing the Other. That of God within knows that we are supposed to be living in the Beloved Community, but our sin is that we turn away from each other. We distance ourselves from our instincts toward love and humanity and we cut off our compassion and empathy.

I used to walk a mile from the train to the community mental health center where I worked downtown, and the number of people experiencing homelessness that I passed by was overwhelming. At the clinic I could see them one by one, but here I was confronted with the violence of poverty and society's indifference every day. It was too much for me, especially when my job required me to be present to people's pain for hours on end. It hurt each time someone asked me for money. It especially hurt because I could afford to give one person money—but not to give money to the next nine or ten people I passed as well. It causes grave harm to walk by someone forced to beg for money on the street and not help. We tell ourselves that the city should fund public housing, that this is the real harm—but both are harmful in their failure to respond. Both gag the piece of the soul that responds with natural compassion and empathy. I started to put in my headphones, avoid eye contact, and try not to see people as I walked.

Then one day shortly into my pregnancy, I saw a young woman sitting at a corner with a sign that said "Pregnant—Please Help." That scaffolding of self-protection I'd built by cutting off my empathy turned to ashes, and all the pain of living in a society that is willing to throw people away washed through me. I started crying right there on the street corner, so aware of the precariousness of life and my good fortune. It is harmful to keep gagging our impulses toward community; it is harmful to ignore suffering. When we cut ourselves off from our own humanity, the other person suffers first and most—but we suffer as well. Moreover, like Sarah, in being willing to deny the other's humanity and rights, we set up a system in which our own humanity and rights will not be respected.

When we are collectively willing to throw away human lives in terrible educational systems, poverty, and prisons, we create an ideology that is willing to throw away human lives—in pointless wars, for example. It's the same ideology of cutting ourselves off from compassion for the Other that puts immigrant babies in cages, that then expands to letting hundreds of thousands of people die needlessly of COVID-19.

What we do to the least of these, we do to *ourselves.*

Queries on Abraham

What are we being called to surrender, so that we can be more fully embraced by God?

How do we discern when obedience is the Spirit-led path and when we are ready for the more mature path of partnership?

Queries on Sarah

Do I follow Abraham's God or Sarah's?

Queries on Hagar

In what ways do we, as a society, repeat the same traumatic compulsions over and over again throughout our history without escaping from the trauma cycle?

In what ways are we each individually and collectively complicit in oppressive systems like predatory capitalism, racism, and sexism? How does that complicity set us up to be victimized ourselves?

How do we interrupt systems of oppression that we are necessarily embedded in? How has God called us to this work in the past, and how is God calling us now?

Queries on Us

How do we ensure we use our individual and collective power in ways that serve the greater good?

If relationships are the site of personal and societal change, how are we led to be in relationship with the people we consider Other or our enemies?

How do we discover and begin to dismantle the premises that white supremacy was founded on? What role does education have in this process? What role does the Spirit have in this process?

How do we root ourselves in our own Truth while being open to being changed by the Truth others carry?

What does living in the Cross look like for you personally? For the Religious Society of Friends today?

Endnotes

1. Marcelle Martin, *Our Life Is Love: The Quaker Spiritual Journey* (San Francisco: Inner Light Books), 120.
2. Micah Bales, "Did God Really Ask Abraham to Sacrifice His Own Child?" https://www.micahbales.com/god-really-ask-abraham-sacrifice-child.
3. Experiment with Light, https://experiment-with-light.org.uk.
4. Margaret Fell, "An Epistle to Convinced but not yet Crucified Friends," 1656. https://www.hallvworthington.com/Margaret_Fox_Selections/MargaretMiscLetters.html.
5. Dan Simmons, *The Fall of Hyperion* (New York: Bantam, 1991).
6. Philip Gulley, "The God of Sarah," https://www.philipgulley.com/the-god-of-sarah.
7. I am indebted to Peterson Toscano and Liam Hooper, two queer Bible scholars whose podcast examines Bible stories through a queer lens, for developing my understanding of this story in their Bible Bash podcast Ep #1, "Ishmael and Hagar – Genesis 16 and 21." *Editors' note:* "Queer" is a term that some on the LGBTQIA spectrum have reclaimed. The author self-identifies as queer, as do Peterson and Liam. Those who are not LGBTQIA should use the word with caution given its history as a slur.
8. Later this is revealed to be true, adding incest to the list of damaging dynamics in this family.
9. A term coined by philosopher-theologian Josiah Royce, who founded the Fellowship of Reconciliation, and popularized and deepened by Dr. Martin Luther King Jr. From the Martin Luther King, Jr. Center for Nonviolent Social Change: "Dr. King's Beloved Community is a global vision, in which all people can share in the wealth of the earth. In the Beloved Community, poverty, hunger and homelessness will not be tolerated because international standards of human decency will not allow it. Racism and all forms of discrimination, bigotry and prejudice will be replaced by an all-inclusive spirit of sisterhood and brotherhood. In the Beloved Community, international disputes will be resolved by peaceful conflict-resolution and reconciliation of adversaries, instead of military power. Love and trust will triumph over fear and hatred. Peace with justice will prevail over war and military conflict." https://thekingcenter.org/about-tkc/the-king-philosophy.
10. Lesbian, Gay, Bisexual, Transgender, Queer, Intersex, and Asexual.
11. George Fox et al., "A Declaration from the harmless and innocent people of God, called Quakers" (London, 1660). www.qhpress.org/quakerpages/qwhp/dec1660.htm.